The Silly Book of Jokes

HAHA

Published in 2016
by Igloo Books Ltd
Cottage Farm
Sywell
NN6 0BJ
www.igloobooks.com

LEO002 0916
4 6 8 10 9 7 5
ISBN 978-1-78343-347-6

Printed and manufactured in China

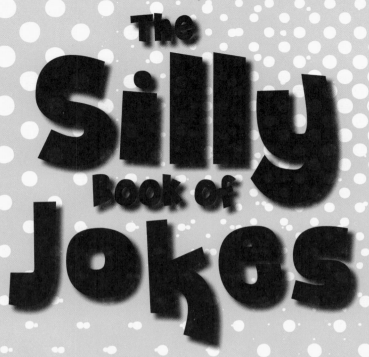

The Silly Book of Jokes

Haaaa!

HEHE

igloobooks

THIS IGLOO BOOK
BELONGS TO:

Uzmadaqueen - Uzma

Haha

HILARIOUS CONTENTS

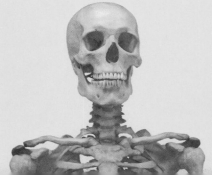

SILLY JOKES

Haaaa!

Hee Heeee!

ALL SORTS OF SILLINESS

This book contains all sorts of silliness. You'll be in awe of the amount of silly jokes, puns, gags and one-liners. We have packed every kind of silliness into this book, from silly animals to silly history and everything in between. Silly. Really very silly.

We all know that there are two kinds of jokes in this world: silly ones and non-silly ones. We've rejected all the non-silly ones and just compiled the silly ones for you to enjoy. It's nice not having to worry about non-silly jokes sneaking in.

Some jokes will make you laugh out loud. Others will make you snigger. Some might make you smirk, while others will bring a huge smile to your face. Silly jokes are silly in many different ways.

Ha!

SILLY JOKES

Speaking of silly, it's time to get stuck into some jokes. One of the best things about the jokes in this book is telling them to your family and friends. You will have them in stitches in no time. What's more awesome than that?

Did You Know?

Silly jokes have been found to help people complete their household chores quicker than non-silly jokes.

I wish I knew some silly jokes I could tell my friends...

I wish someone would tell a silly joke right now...

SILLY ANIMALS

Animals are truly funny creatures. These jokes will have your sides splitting and your ribs tickling.

LOL!

Why did the fox cross the road?

To look for the chicken.

What food do hedgehogs like most?

Prickled onions.

What do you call
a bird in winter?

A brrrd.

Why did the goose
cross the road?

To have a gander
on the other side.

Haaaa!

Why couldn't
Bob ride a bike?

Because Bob's
a fish.

What do you
call a donkey with
only three legs?

A wonkey.

Ha!

How do you catch a squirrel?

Climb a tree and act like a nut.

Where do sheep get their hair cut?

At the baa-baas, of course.

Haaaa!

What kind of fish goes well with ice cream?

Jellyfish.

Which dance will a chicken not do?

The foxtrot.

What did the horse say when it fell?

"I've fallen and I can't giddy-up."

Ha!

What do you call a bird that is out of breath?

A puffin.

Why are fish easy to weigh?

They have their own scales.

LOL!

How do you save a drowning mouse?

Give it mouse-to-mouse resuscitation.

What kind of animal goes, 'Oom'?

A cow walking backwards.

Haaaa!

What did the parakeet say when he finished shopping?

"Just put it on my bill."

What does a farmer talk about when milking cows?

Udder nonsense.

LOL!

Ha! Hee Heeee!

What do you call a rooster who wakes up at the same time every morning?

An alarm cluck.

How do you stop a dog from digging up your garden?

Take away its spade.

Why did the chicken join the band?

Because he had the drumsticks.

Ha!

What do you get if you pour boiling water down a rabbit hole?

Hot cross bunnies.

How does a chicken tell the time?

One o'cluck, two o'cluck, three o'cluck.

Haaaa!

What do you get when a chicken lays an egg on top of a barn?

An egg roll.

What do you call a cow that eats your grass?

A lawn-mooer.

SILLY ANIMALS

Patient: "Doctor, doctor, I keep thinking I'm a sheep."

Doctor: "Really? How do you feel about that?"

Patient: "Really baaaaaaaaaaadd."

What's the best way to brush your hare?

Hold him firmly by his long ears and brush gently.

What do you get if you cross a hen with a dog?

Pooched eggs.

Ha! Hee Heeee!

Ha!

What animal keeps the best time?

A watchdog.

Why are elephants inappropriate when they go swimming?

They can't keep their trunks up.

LOL!

What did the farmer call his two rows of cabbages?

A dual cabbage way.

How do mice celebrate when they move into a new hole?

They have a mouse-warming party.

Haaaa!

What do you call a pony with a cough?

A little hoarse.

Ha!

Why did the bee go
to the doctor?

It had hives.

What is black
and white and lives
in Hawaii?

A lost penguin.

How do fleas travel?

They itchhike.

Did you hear about the
pig with a rash?

He needed a little
oinkment.

LOL!

SILLY JOKES

Why did the worm sleep in?

Because it didn't want to get caught by the early bird.

Who stole the soap?

The robber ducky.

What's black, white and green?

A seasick zebra.

Ha!

Why don't centipedes play football?

By the time they put their shoes on, the game would be over.

Ha! Hee Heeee!

SCARY AND SILLY

Get ready for some freaky frights with these silly, scary jokes. You will love making your friends cackle with these puns, especially around Hallowe'en.

LOL!

What do you call two witches who live together?

Broom-mates.

Ha! Hee Heeee!

What happened when the wizard met the witch?

It was love at first fright.

What kind of mistakes do ghosts make?

Boo-boos.

Why did Dracula take up acting?

It was in his blood.

Ha!

Was Dracula ever married?

No, he was a lifelong bat-chelor.

What dessert do ghosts like the most?

Boo-berry pie.

Haaaa!

LOL!

What should you say when meeting a ghost?

"How do you boo?"

Why are skeletons so calm?

Because nothing gets under their skin.

Ha! Hee Heeee!

Why didn't Jason believe the ghost's lie?

Because he could see right through him.

SILLY JOKES

Why did the
witch itch?

Because someone
took away the 'W'.

What do you get
when a vampire bites
a plumber?

A bloodbath.

LOL!

What did the alien
say to the book?

"Take me to
your reader."

What is a vampire's
food of choice?

Fang-furters.

Ha!

What sound does a witch's breakfast make?

Snap, crackle and pop.

Ha! Hee Heeee!

What scary creature writes invisible books?

A ghost writer.

Haaaa!

What do monsters eat for breakfast?

Devilled eggs.

What happened to Ray when he was eaten by a monster?

He became an ex-Ray.

Where do ghosts buy their food?

At the ghost-ery shop.

Why did the monster's coffee taste like dirt?

It was just ground this morning.

SCARY AND SILLY

LOL!

Haaaa!

What fruit do vampires like the most?

Neck-tarines.

Who gave the lecture at the ghost convention?

The spooksperson.

Ha!

Where is the best place to speak to a monster?

From a long way off.

What do you call
a warlock who tries
to stop fights?

A peacelock.

Why is the letter
'V' like a monster?

It comes after you.

Where do ghosts
and skeletons like
to swim?

In the Dead Sea.

Haaaa!

Why did the witch put her broom in the washing machine?

Because she wanted a clean sweep.

Why did the skeleton play the piano?

Because he didn't have an organ.

LOL!

What did the mother ghost say to the baby ghost?

"Go and put your boos and shocks on."

LOL!

Why do vampires need mouthwash?

Because they have bat breath.

Ha!

What happened when the wizard turned a boy into a hare?

He wouldn't stop rabbiting on about it.

Who did the wizard marry?

His ghoul-friend.

Haaaa!

Why are most mummies vain and conceited?

They are all wrapped up in themselves.

SPORTY SILLINESS

The sporting arena might not seem a likely place to set silly jokes, but just you wait. This chapter is full of silly, sporty fun.

Ha!

What sport do mosquitoes play?

Skin diving.

LOL!

How come the team of artists never won a hockey match?

Because they kept drawing.

SILLY JOKES

What has 22 feet and two wings, but can't fly?

A football team.

Why did the golfer pack an extra pair of pants?

In case he got a hole in one.

Ha!

How do you start a flea race?

Say, "One, two, flea, go."

Haaaa!

What sport do bees like to play?

Rug-bee.

Which game
do elephants play
with ants?

Squash.

What sport do vampires
play together?

Bat-minton.

Ha!

What do cricketers
and magicians have
in common?

They both
do hat tricks.

How do you make
a cream puff?

Chase it around
the backyard.

Haaaa!

SILLY JOKES

Why can't you play sports in the jungle?

Because there are too many cheetahs.

Ha!

What lights up a football stadium?

A football match.

Haaaa!

Why did the baseball coach spill the lemonade?

There was something wrong with the pitcher.

Which dessert does gymnastics?

The banana split.

How do hens encourage their football team?

They egg them on.

Haaaa!

Why are spiders such good swimmers?

Because they have webbed feet.

Why did the tightrope walker visit the bank?

To check his balance.

LOL!

Why didn't the dog want to play tennis?

Because he was a boxer.

SILLY JOKES

What's the hardest part about skydiving?

The ground.

Haaaa!

Why shouldn't you tell jokes while ice skating?

Because the ice might crack up.

Why are basketball players so messy?

Because of all the dribbling.

Ha!

Which insect makes a terrible goalkeeper?

The fumble bee.

Haaaa!

Do you go
rock climbing?

I would if I
were boulder.

Ha!
Hee
Heeeee!

What do you call a
frozen bike?

B-b-b-bicycle.

LOL!

Why did the cricket
team hire a cook?

They needed
a good batter.

Why couldn't Robin
play cricket?

Because he lost
his bat, man.

How can you stop squirrels from playing cricket in the garden?

Hide the ball. It drives them nuts.

LOL!

Why couldn't the bicycles stand up?

Because they were two tyred.

What did the baseball glove say to the baseball?

"Catch you later."

Ha!

Why did all the bowling pins sit down?

Because they were on strike.

Why did the football quit the team?

It was tired of being kicked around.

Why are fish bad at tennis?

Because they don't like getting close to the net.

Ha!

Why couldn't the tennis player light a fire?

Because he had lost all of his matches.

Why did the chicken get a red card?

Because of her fowl play.

LOL!

What game did the roadkill like to play?

Squash.

SILLY JOKES

What tea do football players drink?

Penal-tea.

When is cricket a crime?

When there's a hit and run.

Ha! Hee Heeee!

Haaaa!

Which athlete stays the warmest?

The long jumper.

What happened to the man with a fear of hurdles?

He got over it.

SILLY BIRTHDAYS

Birthday parties are the perfect time to make your friends roll around with laughter. What's more fitting than telling them silly jokes about birthdays?

Ha! Hee Heeee!

LOL!

Johnny: "I get heartburn every time I eat birthday cake."

Mike: "Well, take the candles off next time."

Was anybody famous born on your birthday?

No, only babies were born on my birthday.

SILLY JOKES

Matt: "When's your birthday?"

Will: "22nd of March."

Matt: "What year?"

Will: "Every year."

Ha!

What do you call an adult balloon?

A blown-up.

LOL!

What's the best kind of birthday present?

Another one.

Dylan: "Did you go to Megan's birthday?"

Sally: "No, the invite said '4 to 8' and I'm 9."

KNOCK-KNOCK.

Who's there?

Wanda.

Wanda who?

Wanda wish you a happy birthday.

Ha!

Sam: "Well, I guess my birthday wish didn't come true."

Amanda: "How do you know?"

Sam: "You're still here."

What did the big candle say to the little candle?

"You're too young to go out."

LOL!

SILLY JOKES

Haaaa!

How can you tell that birthdays are good for you?

Because statistics show that the people who have the most birthdays live the longest.

Ha! Hee Heeee!

KNOCK-KNOCK.

Who's there?

Abby.

Abby who?

Abby Birthday to you.

What do you get every birthday?

A year older.

Why do we put candles on the top of birthday cakes?

Because it would be too hard to put them on the bottom.

Ha!

SILLY BIRTHDAYS

Haaaa!

What does every happy birthday end with?

The letter 'Y'.

What is the left side of a birthday cake?

The side that's not eaten.

LOL!

Why did Emma stand on her head at the birthday party?

They were having upside-down cake.

Did you hear about the tree's birthday?

It was a sappy one.

Ha! Hee Heeee!

What do you say to a cow on her birthday?

"Happy birthday to moo."

Ha!

Haaaa!

Why did Tommy hit his birthday cake with a hammer?

It was a pound cake.

What did the birthday cake say to the ice cream?

"You're cool."

LOL!

LOL!

What did the elephant wish for on his birthday?

A trunkful of presents.

What did the ice cream say to the unhappy cake?

"Hey, what's eating you?"

Ha! Hee Heeee!

Ha!

What did the birthday balloon say to the pin?

"Hi, Buster."

What did one candle say to another candle?

"Don't birthdays burn you up?"

LOL!

LOL!

Haaaa!

What does a clam do on his birthday?

He shellabrates.

What birthday cake did the elf eat?

Shortcake.

What was the average age of a caveman?

Stone Age.

SILLY BIRTHDAYS

What has wings, a long tail and wears a bow?

A birthday pheasant.

Ha!

Ha! Hee Heeee!

Where do you find a birthday present for a cat?

In a cat-alogue.

Haaaa!

What party game do rabbits like to play?

Musical hares.

Why was the birthday cake as hard as a rock?

It was marble cake.

SILLY JOKES

What kind of music do balloons hate?

Pop music.

Does a pink candle burn longer than a blue one?

No, they both burn shorter.

LOL!

LOL!

Joel: "Why didn't you get me anything for my birthday?"

Zach: "You told me to surprise you."

SILLY OUTER SPACE

These silly jokes about outer space are truly out of this world. Get ready to blast off into a galaxy of the silliest jokes you could possibly imagine.

LOL!

Why was the alien such a good gardener?

Because he had green fingers.

Haaaa!

What holds the moon up in the sky?

Moonbeams.

SILLY JOKES

Why did the scientist disconnect his doorbell?

He wanted to win the No-bell Prize.

How do you get a baby astronaut to sleep?

Rock-et.

Ha!

LOL!

Where do Martians go for a drink?

Mars bars.

What did E.T.'s parents say to him when he got home?

"Where on Earth have you been?"

Haaaa!

What did Mars say to Saturn?

"Give me a ring some time."

Ha! Hee Heeee!

What did the astronaut see in the frying pan?

An unidentified frying object.

How does a Martian know he's attractive?

When bits of metal stick to him.

Why don't astronauts get hungry after being blasted into space?

Because they just had a big launch.

Haaaa!

What game do spacemen play?

Astronauts and crosses.

Ha!

Where do aliens leave their flying saucers?

At parking meteors.

Haaaa!

Ha!

How did the solar system keep its trousers up?

With an asteroid belt.

Why did the spaceship land outside the bedroom?

Someone had left the landing light on.

Why did the Martian go to the optician?

He had stars in his eyes.

LOL!

Haaaa!

Why did the alien wear a bulletproof vest?

Because of all the shooting stars.

What do you call a wizard from outer space?

A flying sorcerer.

Ha!

What did the alien say to the gardener?

"Take me to your weeder."

What did one shooting star say to the other?

"Pleased to meteor."

Where do aliens keep their sandwiches?

In a launch box.

How does the moon cut his hair?

Eclipse it.

What is the middle of gravity?

The letter 'V'.

Ha!

How do you know when the moon has had enough to eat?

When it's full.

Why did the Sun go to school?

To get brighter.

LOL!

What do planets like to read?

Comet books.

What do you call a tick on the moon?

A luna-tick.

SILLY JOKES

What key do astronauts play on the keyboard?

The space bar.

Why did the cow go to outer space?

To visit the Milky Way.

Ha!

What did the alien say to the cat?

"Take me to your litter."

Why did Venus have to get an air conditioner?

Because Mercury moved in.

Haaaa!

Why didn't people like the restaurant on the moon?

Because it had no atmosphere.

Why couldn't the astronaut book a room on the moon?

Because it was full.

How many astronomers does it take to change a light bulb?

None. Astronomers aren't scared of the dark.

How do astronauts serve dinner?

On flying saucers.

Ha!

Why didn't the Sun go to university?

Because it already had a million degrees.

Ha! Hee Heeee!

What do you get if you cross Santa with a spaceship?

U-F-ho-ho-ho.

How do you get ready for a space party?

You planet.

LOL!

THE SILLY HUMAN BODY

The human body can do truly amazing things, but it can also do truly hilarious things, too.

What has a bottom at its top?

A leg.

Haaaa!

Ha!

What happened when the two red blood cells fell in love?

They loved in vein.

What should you do if you split your sides laughing?

Run until you get a stitch.

Ha!

LOL!

How do you stop a cold going to your chest?

Tie a knot in your neck.

Tom: "I just swallowed a bone."

Ian: "Are you choking?"

Tom: "No, I'm serious."

Ha! Hee Heeee!

LOL!

How long can you live without a brain?

Well, how old are you?

What did one ear say to the other?

"Between us, we have brains."

LOL!

Patient: "Doctor, doctor, I think I'm a battery."

Doctor: "How do you feel about it?"

Patient: "Well, it has its pluses and minuses."

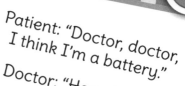

What makes music on your hair?

A headband.

What's the most musical bone?

The trom-bone.

Ha!

Patient: "Doctor, doctor, I've lost my memory."

Doctor: "When did this happen?"

Patient: "When did what happen?"

Haaaa!

What's the best thing to put in a pie?

Your teeth.

63

THE SILLY HUMAN BODY

What do you call a woman with one leg longer than the other?

I-lean.

Haaaa!

Why are snakes not hard to fool?

You can't pull their leg.

LOL!

What smells the best at dinner?

Your nose.

LOL!

Billy: "I don't think I need a spine."

Lucy: "Why is that?"

Billy: "It's holding me back."

Patient: "Doctor, doctor, I keep seeing double."

Doctor: "Take a seat on the couch."

Patient: "Which one?"

Haaaa!

"Doctor, doctor, I think I need glasses."

"You certainly do. This is a fish and chip shop."

Who won the skeleton beauty contest?

No body.

Pete: "Doctor, doctor, I got a strawberry stuck up my bum."

Doctor: "You're in luck. I have cream for that."

Ha! Hee Heeee!

Haaaa!

What kind of flower grows on your face?

Two lips.

Why do skeletons hate winter?

Because the cold goes right through them.

SILLY JOKES

What do you call a skeleton who won't get up in the mornings?

Lazy bones.

How did the skeleton know it was going to rain?

She could feel it in her bones.

Ha! Hee Heeee!

Why do skeletons like to drink milk?

Because milk is so good for the bones.

LOL!

Haaaa!

What do you call a judge with no thumbs?

Justice fingers.

Why did the one-handed man cross the road?

To get to the second-hand shop.

LOL!

What kind of bandages do people wear after heart surgery?

Ticker tape.

Ha!

DINOSAUR SILLINESS

It has been a long time since dinosaurs ruled the Earth and we don't know if they liked silly jokes or not. Given how cool they looked, we think they must have.

Haaaa!

What has a spiked tail and sixteen wheels?

A stegosaurus on roller skates.

Ha!

Why did the dinosaur bathe?

To get ex-stinked.

SILLY JOKES

What do you get when a dinosaur sneezes?

Out of the way.

Ha!

What followed the dinosaurs?

Their tails.

LOL!

How did dinosaurs pass their exams?

With extinction.

What do you call a blind dinosaur?

Do-you-think-he-saurus.

Haaaa!

DINOSAUR SILLINESS

What do you call a dinosaur wearing tight shoes?

My-foot-is-saurus.

Why did the dinosaur cross the road?

Because the chicken didn't exist yet.

Ha!

What does a dinosaur get from scrubbing floors?

Dino-sores.

LOL!

What does a T-rex eat?

Anything he wants.

Why are there old dinosaur bones in the museum?

Because they can't afford to buy new ones.

SILLY JOKES

Which is the scariest dinosaur?

The terror-dactyl.

What do you call a dinosaur that won't stop talking?

A dino-bore.

Ha!

LOL!

Why did the dinosaur go on a diet?

He was too big for his scales.

73

DINOSAUR SILLINESS

How does a T-rex greet you?

"Pleased to eat you."

LOL!

Why do dinosaurs eat raw meat?

Because they don't know how to cook.

What do you call a sleeping dinosaur?

A dino-snore.

Ha!

SILLY JOKES

How did the dinosaur feel after eating a pillow?

A little bit down in the mouth.

Ha!

What did the triceratops sit on?

His tricera-bottom.

LOL!

What should you do if you see a blue dinosaur?

Try to cheer him up.

What do you get when dinosaurs crash their cars?

Tyrannosaurus wrecks.

DINOSAUR SILLINESS

What do you call a dinosaur that likes playing with blocks?

Stack-o-saurus.

What is a dinosaur's lucky number?

Ate.

LOL!

HAaaa!

What did the caveman say when he slid down the dinosaur's neck?

"So long."

How do you invite a dinosaur to dinner?

"Tea, Rex?"

What makes more noise than a dinosaur?

Two dinosaurs.

How did the dinosaur blow up her garage?

With dino-mite.

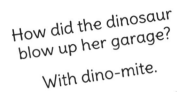

Ha!

What do you call a dinosaur that never gives up?

Try-hard-ceratops.

Why did the T-rex like to eat snowmen?

Because they melted in his mouth.

DINOSAUR SILLINESS

Ha! Hee Heeee!

What happened when the diplodocus took the train home?

He had to bring it back.

What's smarter than a talking dinosaur?

A spelling bee.

LOL!

LOL!

What did the brontosaurus say to the pterodactyl?

"Why the long face?"

What brand of t-shirts do dinosaurs wear?

Tricera-tops.

Ha!

LOL!

What did the doctor say to the invisible dinosaur?

"Sorry, I can't see you right now."

How can you tell there's a stegosaurus in your fridge?

The door won't close.

Haaaa!

FOOD IS SILLY

Food, glorious food. It's delicious and hilarious and very silly. Take a bite out of this special brand of silliness.

How do you know that carrots are good for your eyes?

Because you never see rabbits wearing glasses.

LOL!

LOL!

What did the apple skin say to the apple?

"I've got you covered."

SILLY JOKES

Why did the man get fired from the banana factory?

Because he threw out all the bent ones.

Ha!

What type of nut is made from bread?

A doughnut.

LOL!

Why did the jelly wobble?

Because it saw the milk shake.

Why was the man swimming in a bowl of muesli?

A strong currant had pulled him in.

FOOD IS SILLY

Why did the
bacon laugh?

Because the egg
cracked a yolk.

Why did the idiot
eat biscuits?

He was crackers.

What do sea
monsters eat?

Fish and ships.

Ha!
Hee
Heeee!

LOL!

What do you call
cheese that isn't yours?

Nacho cheese.

What do you call
shoes made from
banana peels?

Slippers.

What do drummers have for dinner?

Chicken drumsticks.

What's green and white and jumps up and down?

A frog sandwich.

Haaaa!

Why did the cucumber need a lawyer?

Because she was in a pickle.

What did baked beans do to Doug's stomach?

They rectum.

FOOD IS SILLY

Where do baby apes sleep?

In apricots.

Haaaa!

What did one plate say to the other plate?

"Lunch is on me."

Did you hear the joke about the jam?

I won't tell you because it might spread.

LOL!

What do you call a bunch of dolls standing in a row?

A Barbie queue.

SILLY JOKES

What did the
chewing gum say
to the shoe?

"I'm stuck on you."

What do you call
an angry pea?

Grump-pea.

LOL!

What do sheep have
for Christmas lunch?

Baa-becue food.

What's red and
goes up and down?

A tomato
in a lift.

FOOD IS SILLY

Why did the boy throw butter into the sky?

He wanted to see a butterfly.

Why couldn't the burger stop making jokes?

It was on a roll.

What kind of bear has a sweet tooth?

A gummi bear.

What is square and green?

A lemon in disguise.

Why aren't bananas ever lonely?

Because they come in bunches.

What do you call a retired vegetable?

A has-bean.

LOL!

Ha!

Which vegetable goes best with jacket potatoes?

Button mushrooms.

Why did the tomato go out with the prune?

Because he couldn't find a date.

How can you make a chicken stew?

Keep it waiting for hours.

What did the tin say to the tin opener?

"You make me flip my lid."

LOL!

Why did the apple cry?

Its peelings were hurt.

How do you make a banana split?

Cut it in half.

How do you make an apple puff?

Chase it around the garden for hours.

SILLY JOKES

What did the toaster say to the loaf?

"Pop up and see me sometime."

What did the mayonnaise say to the fridge?

"Go away. I'm dressing."

Why did the cookie go to the hospital?

He felt crumby.

Ha!

What cheese is made backwards?

Edam.

What can a whole orange do that a half orange can't?

Look round.

Haaaa!

HOW SILLY IS HISTORY?

History may have happened a long time ago, but that doesn't make it any less hysterical.

Ha! Hee Heeee!

How do you use an Ancient Egyptian doorbell?

Toot and come in.

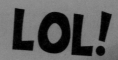

LOL!

Why did Robin Hood only rob the rich?

Because the poor didn't have anything worth stealing.

Which civilisation invented the fountain pen?

The Inkas.

SILLY JOKES

How did Vikings communicate with each other?

They used Norse code.

Where was Henry VIII crowned?

On his head.

Why is history fruity?

Because it's full of dates.

Who was the fastest runner in history?

Adam. He was first in the human race.

Where did the pilgrims land when they came to America?

On their feet.

LOL!

What was the speed limit in Ancient Egypt?

Forty Niles an hour.

What do you get if you cross the Atlantic with the *Titanic*?

Halfway.

Ha!

How do we know that Rome was built in a night?

History tells us it wasn't built in a day.

How does Moses make tea?

Hebrews it.

Haaaa!

Why did Henry VIII have so many wives?

He liked to chop and change.

Which was the most reasonable pharoah in Egypt?

Pharoah Nuff.

Ha!

What happened to Lady Godiva's horse when he found out she wasn't wearing any clothes?

It made him shy.

LOL!

What did the damsel in distress say to the knight?

"Don't just sit there. Slay something."

SILLY JOKES

John: "I wish I had been alive a few hundred years ago."

Teacher: "Why?"

John: "There would have been a lot less history to learn."

Who invented fire?

Some bright spark.

LOL!

Ha!

Why did the mummy have a holiday?

He wanted to unwind.

Why does history keep repeating itself?

Nobody was listening the first time.

What did the dragon say when he met a knight in shining armour?

"I love tinned food."

HOW SILLY IS HISTORY?

Caesar: "What's the weather like?"

Brutus: "Hail, Caesar."

Why were the early days of history called the Dark Ages?

There were lots of knights.

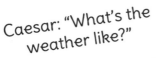

Why did knights in armour practise a lot?

To stop them getting rusty.

How do mummies begin their emails?

Tomb it may concern.

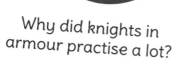

Which monarchs aren't buried in Westminster Abbey?

The ones that are still alive.

Ha!

Who was the most famous French skeleton?

Napoleon bone-apart.

When a knight was killed in battle, what sign did they put on his grave?

Rust in peace.

LOL!

Haaaa!

Why is England the wettest country?

Because the queen has reigned there for years.

98

Where was the Declaration of Independence signed?

At the bottom.

What kind of lighting did Noah use for the ark?

Floodlights.

How was the Roman Empire divided?

With a pair of Caesars.

Who built the ark?

I have Noah idea.

SILLINESS AT SCHOOL

You spend a lot of time at school and it's the perfect place to tell some cracker jokes.

Ha! Hee Heeee!

What do you call a dog that's also a librarian?

A hush puppy.

Why did the music teacher need a ladder?

So she could reach the high notes.

LOL!

Why was the nose sad after the audition?

He didn't get picked.

What are the
longest tables
in the world?

Multiplication tables.

What do you call
a teacher wearing
headphones?

Anything you like.
He can't hear you.

When can school uniforms be fire hazards?

When they are blazers.

What subject do snakes like to learn?

Hiss-tory.

Haaaa!

Why did the baseball player take his bat to the library?

Because his teacher told him to hit the books.

Ha! Hee Heeee!

SILLY JOKES

Why did the science teacher jump in the lake?

He wanted to test the water.

Why was the algebra book sad?

Because it had too many problems.

Teacher: "Why is your exam paper blank?"

Natalie: "I used invisible ink."

Which type of snake is good at its sums?

An adder.

How do you make the number one vanish?

Put a 'G' at the start and it's gone.

LOL!

Teacher: "Why didn't you do your homework, you lazy girl?"

Sarah: "You can't tell me off for something I didn't do."

What did the bookworm say to the school librarian?

"Please can I burrow this book?"

Haaaa!

What happened to the plant in the classroom?

It grew square roots.

LOL!

Why are fish really smart?

Because they live in schools.

What did the ruler say to the pencil?

"You're looking pretty sharp today."

Why was the teacher so good at teaching Geography?

He had abroad knowledge of his subject.

Haaaa!

LOL!

What did the page say to the cover?

"You're squishing me."

"My teacher doesn't know anything. All she does is ask questions."

How did the geography student drown?

His grades were below C-level.

Ha!

What did the pen say to the paper?

"Are you sure that's the write answer?"

Teacher: "What do you get if you multiply 5689 by 20?"

Eva: "The wrong answer."

SILLINESS AT SCHOOL

How do bees get to school?

By school buzz.

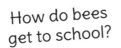

Ha!

What do you call a teacher who has fallen asleep in the classroom?

Nothing. You might wake him up.

LOL!

What do you call a rock that doesn't show up for school?

A skipping stone.

Teacher: "You missed school yesterday, didn't you?"

Student: "No, not very much."

Ha!

Why did the teacher wear dark glasses?

Because the class was so bright.

Why should you avoid doing your sums?

Because if you add four and four, you'll get ate.

KNOCK-KNOCK SILLINESS

You know how they work. Find the ones you like the most and impress your friends with all these silly KNOCK-KNOCK jokes.

KNOCK-KNOCK.

Who's there?

Hatch.

Hatch who?

Bless you.

LOL!

KNOCK-KNOCK.

Who's there?

Doowie.

Doowie who?

Doowie have to go to school?

LOL!

KNOCK-KNOCK.

Who's there?

Doctor.

Doctor who?

No, he's in the Tardis at the moment.

KNOCK-KNOCK.

Who's there?

Harry.

Harry who?

Harry up and open this door.

KNOCK-KNOCK.

Who's there?

Isabel.

Isabel who?

Isabel necessary on a bicycle?

SILLY JOKES

KNOCK-KNOCK.

Who's there?

Banana.

Banana who?

KNOCK-KNOCK.

Who's there?

Banana.

Banana who?

KNOCK-KNOCK.

Who's there?

Banana.

Banana who?

KNOCK-KNOCK.

Who's there?

Orange.

Orange who?

Orange you glad I didn't say banana?

KNOCK-KNOCK SILLINESS

KNOCK-KNOCK.

Who's there?

Cows go.

Cows go who?

No, cows go moo.

KNOCK-KNOCK.

Who's there?

Arthur.

Arthur who?

Arthur got.

KNOCK-KNOCK.

Who's there?

Roach.

Roach who?

Roach you a letter. Did you get it?

KNOCK-KNOCK.

Who's there?

A herd.

A herd who?

A herd you were home,
so I came over.

KNOCK-KNOCK.

Who's there?

Adore.

Adore who?

Adore is between us.
Open up.

Haaaa!

KNOCK-KNOCK.

Who's there?

Ben.

Ben who?

Ben knocking for ten minutes now.

Haaaa!

KNOCK-KNOCK.

Who's there?

Lettuce.

Lettuce who?

Lettuce in.
It's cold out here.

LOL!

KNOCK-KNOCK.

Who's there?

Canoe.

Canoe who?

Canoe help me with my homework?

Ha!

Haaaa!

KNOCK-KNOCK.

Who's there?

Woo.

Woo who?

Woo-hoo to you, too.

KNOCK-KNOCK.

Who's there?

Aida.

Aida who?

Aida sandwich for lunch today.

SILLY JOKES

KNOCK-KNOCK.

Who's there?

Howard.

Howard who?

Howard I know?

KNOCK-KNOCK.

Who's there?

Interrupting cow.

Interrupting co-

MOOOOOO.

Ha! Hee Heeee!

Haaaa!

KNOCK-KNOCK.

Who's there?

Noah.

Noah who?

Noah good
knock-knock joke?

KNOCK-KNOCK.

Who's there?

Eileen.

Eileen who?

Eileen on you,
you lean on me.

RIDDLE ME SILLY

Riddles are lots of fun to solve and we have chosen the silliest riddles, just for you. The answers to the riddles in this chapter are on pages 128 and 129.

LOL!

1. What runs, but never walks?

2. How many months of the year have 28 days?

3. What's black when it's clean and white when it's dirty?

4. What gets bigger the more you take away?

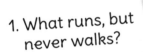
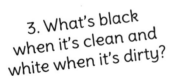
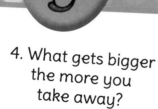
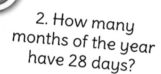

5. What has a head and a tail, but no body?

LOL!

6. What is full of holes, but can still hold water?

7. What goes up, but never comes down?

8. What can you serve, but not eat?

9. What nut has no shell?

10. What goes up and down, but doesn't move?

11. What has one head and one foot, but four legs?

Ha!

12. What runs around a field without moving?

LOL!

13. What's yours, but others use it more than you do?

Ha! Hee Heeeee!

14. What can you make that can't be seen?

15. What do you get after it's been taken?

16. What needs to be answered, but doesn't ask a question?

LOL!

17. What ring is shaped like a square?

18. What room has no floors, no walls and no windows?

19. What gets wetter the more it dries?

20. What five letter word becomes shorter when you add two letters to it?

21. What is no sooner spoken than broken?

22. What runs forever, but never moves at all?

23. What is not alive, but grows and needs air?

24. When things go wrong, what can you always count on?

LOL!

Ha!

25. What smells bad when it's alive, but delicious when it's dead?

26. What is it that you can keep after giving it to somebody else?

LOL!

27. What is as round as a dishpan, deep as a tub, but couldn't be filled up by an ocean?

Haaaa!

28. What goes round the house and in the house, but never touches the house?

29. What is put on a table and cut, but never eaten?

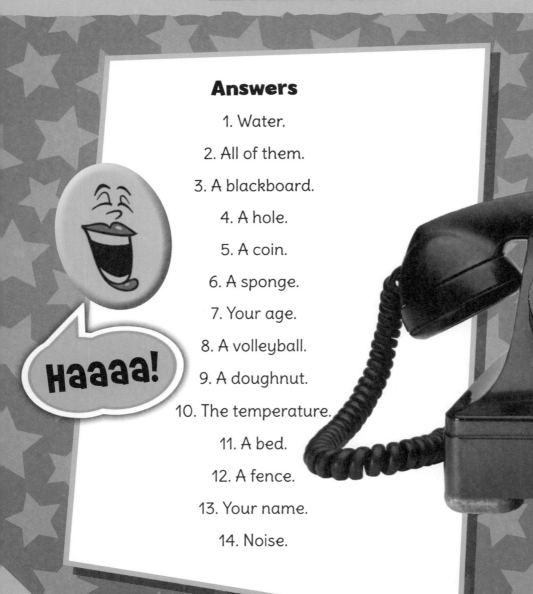

Answers

1. Water.

2. All of them.

3. A blackboard.

4. A hole.

5. A coin.

6. A sponge.

7. Your age.

8. A volleyball.

9. A doughnut.

10. The temperature.

11. A bed.

12. A fence.

13. Your name.

14. Noise.

Haaaa!

15. A photo.

16. A telephone.

17. A boxing ring.

18. A mushroom.

19. A towel.

20. Short.

21. Silence.

22. A waterfall.

23. Fire.

24. Your fingers.

25. Bacon.

26. Your word.

27. A sieve.

28. The Sun.

29. A deck of cards.

VERY SILLY TONGUE-TWISTERS

You are going to need to warm up your tongue to wrap it around some of these. They're twisty and tricky. Make sure you say them out loud.

LOL!

Peter Piper picked a peck of pickled peppers. A peck of pickled peppers Peter Piper picked. If Peter Piper picked a peck of pickled peppers, where's the peck of pickled peppers Peter Piper picked?

I saw Suzie sitting in a shoe shine shop. Where she sits she shines and where she shines, she sits.

How can a clam cram in a clean cream can?

Denise sees the fleece, Denise sees the fleas. At least Denise could sneeze and feed and freeze the fleas.

Fuzzy Wuzzy was a bear. Fuzzy Wuzzy had no hair. Fuzzy Wuzzy wasn't very fuzzy, was he?

Ha!

She sells seashells by the seashore. The shells she sells are surely seashells. So if she sells shells on the seashore, I'm sure she sells seashore shells.

Haaaa!

You've no need to light a nightlight on a night like tonight, for a nightlight's light's a slight light and tonight's a night that's light. When a night's light, like tonight's light, it is really not quite right to light nightlights with their slight lights on a light night like tonight.

Haaaa!

Ha! Hee Heeee!

A big, black bug bit a big, black bear and made the big, black bear bleed blood.

One-one was a racehorse. Two-two was one, too. When One-one won one race, Two-two won one, too.

Ed had edited it.

Lesser leather never weathered wetter weather better.

A skunk sat on a stump and thunk the stump stunk, but the stump thunk the skunk stunk.

LOL!

Freshly fried fresh flesh.

Can you imagine an imaginary menagerie manager imagining managing an imaginary menagerie?

LOL!

What time does the wristwatch strap shop shut?

LOL!

Old oily Ollie oils old oily autos.

The sixth, sick sheik's sixth, sick sheep.

Kitty caught the kitten in the kitchen.

Ha!

Eleven owls licked eleven, little liquorice lollipops.

Zebras zig and zebras zag.

If two witches were watching two watches, which witch would watch which watch?

The big bug bit the little beetle, but the little beetle bit the big bug back.

The blue bluebird blinks.

A tricky, frisky snake with sixty, super scaly stripes.

SILLY JOKES

Give papa a cup of proper coffee in a copper coffee cup.

Three free throws were thrown on three free throws.

A big, black bug bit a big, black dog on his big, black nose.

Not these things here, but those things there.

Red leather, yellow leather. Red leather, yellow leather.

Quick kiss, quick kiss, quick kiss, quick kiss.

LOL!

Friendly fleas and fireflies. Friendly fleas and fireflies.

Fresh, fried fish, fish fresh fried, fried fish fresh, fish fried fresh.

Can you can a can as a canner can can a can?

LOL!

When a doctor doctors a doctor, does the doctor doing the doctoring doctor as the doctor being doctored wants to be doctored, or does the doctor doing the doctoring doctor as he wants to doctor?

HAVE YOU HEARD THIS SILLY ONE?

Everyone loves a silly joke. Here's a collection of the silliest jokes that don't fit into a particular category. They're just that silly!

LOL!

Have you heard the joke about the dustbin lorry?

Don't worry. It's only a load of rubbish.

Have you heard the joke about the toilet?

Never mind. It's far too dirty.

Ha!

Have you heard the joke about the broken pencil?

Never mind. It's pointless.

Have you heard about the guy whose whole left side was cut off?

He's all right now.

Ha! Hee Heeee!

Have you heard the one about the crow and the telephone pole?

He wanted to make a long-distance caw.

Have you heard about the musician with issues?

He was a trebled man.

Have you heard about the stonemason's son?

He was a chip off the old block.

Have you heard about the fire at the circus?

It was in tents.

LOL!

LOL!

Have you heard about the dinosaur that did rodeo?

He was called Bronco-saurus.

Have you heard that the sausage factory aren't making their sausages any longer?

They were long enough already.

SILLY JOKES

Have you heard
what they call
a baby whale?

A little squirt.

Have you heard about
the plastic surgeon who
sat by the fire?

He melted.

Have you heard about
the carrot that died?

There was a big
turn-up at its funeral.

Have you heard
about the bright student
from another planet?

He went to universe-ity.